Joy

QUOTATIONS FROM THE WRITINGS OF ELLEN G. WHITE

Pacific Press Publishing Association
Boise, Idaho
Oshawa, Ontario, Canada

Cover Photo by Russ Bishop

Copyright 1996
Pacific Press Publishg Association
Printed in United States of America
All Rights Reserved

ISBN 0-8163-1368-7

96 97 98 99 00 • 5 4 3 2 1

INTRODUCTION

While some may think that the Christian life should be characterized by stern solemnity at all times, this is certainly not the picture that we get from reading the Bible or the writings of Ellen White. Jesus said that He had come that we might have life and have it "more abundantly" (John 10:10). The apostle Paul counseled us to "rejoice in the Lord alway," and having said that, he decided it bore repeating—"and again I say rejoice" (Philippians 4:4).

Certainly Christians who know they have a Saviour have much to be joyful about. The quotations compiled here are drawn from the writings of Ellen G. White. In many of her letters and manuscripts she wrote about the source of joy and the pimportance of cheerfulness in all circumstances. She often counseled her readers about how to maintain a spirit of joy even when trials come.

In this book we have drawn together some of the brief statements about joy from her pen. We trust that many who read them will find encouragement, strength, and joy everlasting.—

The Compilers

$\mathcal{J}$oy in the Holy Spirit is health-giving, life-giving joy.
In giving us His Spirit, God gives us Himself,
making Himself a fountain of divine influences,
to give health and life to the world.

7T 273

*O*ur happiness comes not from what is around us,
but from what is within us;
not from what we have, but from what we are.

YI 23 January 1902

A pure, harmonious character, a sunny temper,
reflecting light and cheerfulness,
glorifies God, and benefits humanity.

HR 1 June 1871

$\mathcal{J}$oy which brings no sorrow with it. . . .
is the result of an indwelling Saviour.

TM 390

The joy that was set before Jesus
was that of seeing souls redeemed
by the sacrifice of His glory, His honor,
His riches, and His own life.
The salvation of man was His joy.

2T 686

$\mathscr{C}$arry your duties of today cheerfully.
Today's faith, today's trust in Jesus, we must have.
Today I may look and live.
Today I will put my trust in God.
Today I will rest in quietude and peace
kept by the power of God.
Say, "The Lord will be glorified by my being cheerful
and happy in His assurance of His love—today."

UL 180

$\mathcal{T}$he restraint God's word imposes upon us
is for our own interest.
It increases the happiness of our families,
and all around us.
It refines our taste, sanctifies our judgment,
and brings peace of mind,
and in the end, everlasting life.

4bSG 99

A sense of our weakness and unworthiness
should lead us with humility of heart
to plead the atoning sacrifice of Christ.
As we rely upon His merits
we shall find rest and peace and joy.

5T 200

Those who abide in Jesus
will be happy, cheerful, and joyful in God.
A subdued gentleness will mark the voice,
reverence for spiritual and eternal things
will be expressed in the actions, and music,
joyful music, will echo from the lips,
for it is wafted from the throne of God.

FLB 226

*W*e must let the bright beams
of the Sun of Righteousness shine into our hearts,
that we may reflect light to others.
We may daily be blessed, and be a blessing to others,
promoting love, joy, and peace wherever we go.

RH 18 July 1893

*B*ut do not become discouraged;
cast your care upon God and remain calm and cheerful.
Begin every day with earnest prayer,
not omitting to offer praise and thanksgiving.

TMK 232

*W*e should let cheerfulness and joy be welcomed
to our houses and hearts.
If we do this, our health will be improved,
and our lives of usefulness will be prolonged.

HR 1 April 1871

Parents, let the sunshine
of love, cheer, and happy content enter your own hearts,
and let its sweet influence pervade the home.

AH 426

$\mathcal{D}$o not think to find happiness in selfish amusement.
The flowers thus gathered soon wither and die.
True happiness is found only in the Master's service.
In him who is the Light of the world
we shall find comfort and hope.

YI 23 January 1902

Purity and innocence and conformity
to Christ's character will make heaven enjoyable.
All the faculties will be strengthened, all in harmony.
Perfect bliss can only dwell in the heart
where Christ reigns supreme.

TMK 95

We are not to wait until we shall get into heaven
for brightness and comfort and joy.
We are to have them right here in this life.
I testify to all who love and serve God,
that we miss very much because we do not grasp
the blessings that may be ours in our afflictions.

RH 27 December 1894

*W*hen we can,
notwithstanding disagreeable circumstances,
rest confidingly in His love
and shut ourselves in with Him,
resting peacefully in His love,
the sense of His presence
will inspire a deep, tranquil joy.

ML 184

Many cherish the impression that devotion to God
is detrimental to health and to cheerful happiness
in the social relations of life.
But those who walk in the path of wisdom and holiness. . . .
are alive to the enjoyment of life's real pleasures,
while they are not troubled with vain regrets
over misspent hours. . . .

3 BC 1156

As Jesus opens before them the riches of redemption,
and the amazing achievements
in the great controversy with Satan,
the hearts of the ransomed thrill
with more fervent devotion,
and with more rapturous joy
they sweep the harps of gold.

FLB 10

⚹ *If* such would find true happiness,
their minds must first receive the right discipline.
⚹ They must learn to have faith and confidence in God.

Becho 15 October 1893

Should not Christians publish
throughout the world the joy of serving Christ?
Those who in heaven join with the angelic choir
in their anthem of praise
must learn on earth the song of heaven,
the keynote of which is thanksgiving.

7T 244

A contented mind, a cheerful spirit,
is health to the body and strength to the soul.

1T 702

If youth will feel their responsibility before God,
they will be elevated above everything
that is mean, selfish, and impure. . . .
They will realize that they have something
great and glorious to live for.
This will have an influence . . .
to make them earnest, cheerful, and strong.

ML 161

Cheerfulness and a clear conscience
are better than drugs,
and will be an effective agent
in your restoration to health.

HR 1 June 1871

The Lord would have all His sons and daughters
happy, peaceful, and obedient.
Through the exercise of faith
the believer comes into possession of these blessings.

AA 564

As we realize His great love,
our hearts will be inspired with gratitude,
we shall serve Him with cheerfulness,
and firmly, confidently put our trust wholly in Him.

TDG 116

In Christ is fullness of joy forevermore. ✗
The desires and pleasures and amusements of the world
are never satisfying nor healing to the soul.
But Jesus says, "Whoso eateth My flesh,
and drinketh My blood, hath eternal life."

TM 390

The joy of seeing souls eternally saved
will be the reward of all
who follow in the steps of the Redeemer.

9T 59

God in His providence has willed
that no one can secure happiness
by living for himself alone.
The joy of our Lord consisted
in enduring toil and shame for others,
that they might be benefited thereby.
We are capable of being happy
in following His example
and living to bless our fellow men.

4T 224

A cheerful temper, and a hopeful mind,
will do much to cure the real diseases of the system;
for a cheerful heart vitalizes,
and imparts health to the entire system.

HR 1 July 1872

Christ dwelling in the soul is a wellspring of joy.
For all who receive Him,
the very keynote of the word of God is rejoicing.

COL 162

But the purest joy is not found in riches
nor where covetousness is always craving,
but where contentment reigns
and where self-sacrificing love is the ruling principle.

3T 382

And all the way up the steep road leading to eternal life
are well-springs of joy to refresh the weary.
Those who walk in wisdom's ways are,
even in tribulation, exceeding joyful.

MB 140

We must do our work
with cheerfulness and hopefulness.
We are in no case to become discouraged.
Let us keep our eyes off the disagreeable parts
of our experience, and let our words
be full of good cheer.

SD 218

We are sustained every moment by God's care,
and upheld by His power.
He spreads our tables with food.
He gives us peaceful and refreshing sleep.

CS 18

There are many who,
though striving to obey God's commandments,
have little peace or joy.
This lack in their experience is the result of a failure
to exercise faith. . . .
The Lord would have all His sons and daughters
happy, peaceful, and obedient.

AA 563, 564

It is better to endure cheerfully
every inconvenience
than to part with peace and contentment.

AH 156

While cheerfulness and a calm resignation
and peace will make others happy and healthy,
it will be of the greatest benefit to oneself.

2 MCP 662

Even here we are by faith
to enter into the Saviour's joy.
Like Moses, we are to endure as seeing the Invisible.

MH 504

It is the precious privilege of teachers and parents
to co-operate in teaching the children
how to drink in the gladness of Christ's life
by learning to follow His example.

AH 290

When, relying upon your tried Helper,
you have done all you can, accept the result cheerfully.
It will not always be gain from the worldling's standpoint,
but perhaps success might have been
the worst thing for you.

TMK 232

$\mathcal{L}$ook upon matters in a cheerful light,
seeking to lift the shadows that, if cherished,
will envelop the soul.

AH 433

If we gather to our souls the joys of heaven and,
as far as possible,
express them in our words and deportment,
we shall be more pleasing to our heavenly Father
than if we were gloomy and sad.

AH 430

*W*ords of cheer and encouragement spoken
when the soul is sick and the pulse of courage is low—
these are regarded by the Saviour as if spoken to Himself.

LHU 95

*W*hen we cheerfully take up the small duties
that lie in our pathway, and do them well,
higher and greater responsibilities will be intrusted to us.

ST 23 October 1884

$\mathcal{L}$et vegetation, that is clothed in cheerful green,
cheer and comfort you, and suggest to you the happiness
that you may reflect upon others,
by presenting before them
the aspect of freshness and cheerfulness.

HR 1 June 1871

$\mathcal{L}$et us all forget self as much as possible,
cultivate cheerfulness, seek to brighten the lives of others,
and we shall then have less desire
to complain of our own lot.

HP 273

→ Christ has said that it was his will
that your joy should be full.
Why should you not have fullness of joy,
when through Christ
you have the prospect of eternal life at his coming?

ST 17 March 1890

It is the little attentions,
the numerous small incidents and simple courtesies of life,
that make up the sum of life's happiness;
and it is the neglect of kindly,
encouraging, affectionate words,
and the little courtesies of life,
which helps compose the sum of life's wretchedness.

AH 108

$\mathcal{L}$et us remember that everyone
has some dark spot in his experience.
Let us do all we can to bring cheerfulness and hope
into the lives of others.
What a blessing this will be to them.
In their turn they will speak words of good cheer
to others to bring sunshine into their hearts.

UL 185

Cheerfulness without levity
is one of the Christian graces.

4T 62

The life in which the fear of the Lord is cherished
will not be a life of sadness and gloom.
It is the absence of Christ that makes the countenance sad,
and the life a pilgrimage of sighs.

COL 162

When you surrender yourself entirely to God,
when you fall all broken upon Jesus,
you will be rewarded by a victory the joy
of which you have never yet realized.

GW (1892 ed.) 372, 373

$\mathcal{W}$e can make heaven in heart and home
as we pass along if our lives are hid with Christ in God.
Thus we can bring joy and comfort
into the lives of others. Christ's joy will remain in us,
and our joy will be full.

2SAT 147

Often there will come to us
a sweet joyful sense of the presence of Jesus.
Often our hearts will burn within us as He draws nigh
to commune with us as He did with Enoch.

COL 129

*W*e should be cheerful;
for there is nothing gloomy
in the religion of Jesus.

GW 92

We have a hope
that is far above any pleasure the world can give;
why should we not then be joyful?

ST 11 August 1909

The cheerful enlightenment
of the mind and the soul temple
by the assurance that we have reconciliation with God,
the hope we have of everlasting life through Christ,
and the pleasure of blessing others
are joys which bring no sorrow with them.

HP 245

$\mathcal{T}$he Bible presents to our view
the unsearchable riches and immortal treasures of heaven.
Man's strongest impulse urges him
to seek his own happiness,
and the Bible recognizes this desire
and shows us that all heaven will unite with man
in his efforts to gain true happiness.

AG 363

*B*risk, yet not violent exercise in the open air,
with cheerfulness of spirits, will promote the circulation,
giving a healthful glow to the skin,
and sending the blood, vitalized by the pure air,
to the extremities.

2T 530

As the children of Israel,
journeying through the wilderness,
cheered their way by the music of sacred song,
so God bids His children today
gladden their pilgrim life.

FLB 273

3—JOY

The faces of men and women
who walk and work with God
express the peace of heaven.
They are surrounded with the atmosphere of heaven.
For these souls the kingdom of God has begun.
They have Christ's joy,
the joy of being a blessing to humanity.

DA 312

The Saviour was joyful in the joy He had awakened.
As He witnessed the sufferings of those
who had come to Him,
His heart was stirred with sympathy,
and He rejoiced in His power
to restore them to health and happiness.

DA 259

As hearts are cheered,
the heavenly angels look on in pleased recognition.

LHU 95

It is our privilege to seek constantly
the joy of His presence.
He desires us to be cheerful
and to be filled with praise to His name.

ST 11 August 1909

Cultivate sympathy for others.
Let cheerfulness, kindness, and love pervade the home.
This will increase a love for religious exercises,
and duties large and small
will be performed with a light heart.

AH 433

In some cases the idea has been entertained
that cheerfulness is inconsistent with the dignity
of the Christian character, but this is a mistake.
Heaven is all joy. ←

AH 430

*W*hen we have an assurance,
which is bright and clear, of our own salvation,
we shall exhibit cheerfulness and joyfulness,
which becomes every follower of Jesus Christ.

Ev 630, 631

One pulse of harmony and gladness
beats through the vast creation.
From Him who created all, flow life and light and gladness,
throughout the realms of illimitable space.
From the minutest atom to the greatest world,
all things, animate and inanimate,
in their unshadowed beauty and perfect joy,
declare that God is love.

FLB 10

The fruit of the Spirit is love, joy, and peace.
Discord and strife are the work of Satan
and the fruit of sin.

5T 169

We should be cheerful,
if only for the benefit of those
who depend more or less upon us for happiness.

HP 273

God is the source
of life and light and joy to the universe.
Like rays of light from the sun,
blessings flow out from Him
to all the creatures He has made.

CS 23

$\mathcal{Y}$ou are making a mistake in searching for happiness.
If you find it, it will be in the performance of duty
and the forgetfulness of self.

3T 329

Those who have been long acquainted with God,
who from their youth have drawn
their happiness from the pure fountain of heaven,
are prepared to enter the family of God.

ML 156

We may have joy unspeakable and full of glory.
Let us put away our indolence
and study God's Word more constantly.

Ev 180

As they learn more and more
of the wisdom, the love, and the power of God,
their minds will be constantly expanding,
and their joy will continually increase.

5T 702, 703

It is right to be cheerful, and even joyful.
It is right to cultivate cheerfulness of spirit
through sanctification of the truth;
but it is not right to indulge in foolish jesting and joking,
in lightness and trifling,
in words of criticism and condemnation of others.

7 BC 938

*L*et us keep our eyes off
the disagreeable parts of our experience,
and let our words be full of good cheer.
We can surround ourselves with a sunny atmosphere,
or with an atmosphere charged with gloom.
Let us educate ourselves to talk courage.

SD 218

The way of true happiness
remains the same in all ages.
Patient continuance in well-doing
will lead to honor, happiness, and eternal life.

HR 1 June 1878

The Christian laborer
knows no drudgery in his heaven-appointed work.
He enters into the joy of His Lord
in seeing souls emancipated from the slavery of sin;
and this joy repays him for every self-denial.

ChS 269

If we would enjoy eternal bliss,
we must cultivate religion in the home. . . .
Peace, harmony, affection, and happiness
should be perseveringly cherished every day,
until these precious things abide in the hearts
of those who compose the family

FLB 279

In order for you to be cheerful,
you should have exercise.
You should have something useful to do.

HR 1 June 1871

$\mathcal{L}$ove for God is essential for life and health.
In order to have perfect health
our hearts must be filled with hope and love and joy.

CH 587

$\mathcal{L}$et the evenings be spent as happily as possible.
Let home be a place
where cheerfulness, courtesy, and love exist.

CH 100

Sin is the cause of all our woes.
If we would have true peace and happiness of mind,
sin must be removed.

2MCP 649, 650

We may look up
through the attractive glories of nature,
to nature's glorious God, and,
as we read his love to man in nature,
we may become cheerful, thankful, pure, and holy.

HR 1 May 1871

*L*et us, all who can,
go out of doors, and be cheerful, happy, and healthy,
as we behold the charming beauties of nature.

HR 1 May 1871

On His prayer for His disciples He said,
"And now I come to thee;
and these things I speak in the world,
that they might have my joy fulfilled in themselves."
Is it possible to have joy in obeying Christ?
It is the only real joy that any soul can have.

SD 195

$\mathcal{L}$et there be singing in the home,
  of songs that are sweet and pure,
and there will be fewer words of censure,
and more of cheerfulness and hope and joy.

FLB 273

If you would have peace in your hearts,
you must seek earnestly to imitate the life of Christ.
Then there will be no need of affecting cheerfulness
or of your seeking for pleasure in the indulgence of pride
and the frivolities of the world.

ML 161

We may have true Christian dignity
and at the same time
be cheerful and pleasant in our deportment.

4T 62

$\mathscr{C}$heerfulness and courtesy
should especially be cultivated by parents and teachers.
All may possess a cheerful countenance,
a gentle voice, a courteous manner,
and these are elements of power.

Ed 27

$\mathcal{W}$e cannot be happy
while we are wrapped up in our interest for ourselves.
We should live in this world to win souls to the Saviour.

4T 72

4—JOY

*G*od desired to bring all peoples
under His merciful rule.
He desired that the earth should be filled
with joy and peace.
He created man for happiness,
and He longs to fill human hearts
with the peace of heaven.

COL 290

$\mathcal{W}$e are children of God,
mutually dependent upon one another for happiness. . . .
It is the proper cultivation
of the social elements of our nature
that brings us into sympathy
with our brethren and affords us happiness
in our efforts to bless others.

4T 71

Cultivate quick sympathy;
always have a cheerful, happy face,
and be ready to lend a helping hand
to those who need your aid. . . .
He [God] will make an accurate entry
of every deed done to His glory. . . .
And in the great day of final accounts
you will receive a glorious reward.

SD 149

$\mathcal{D}$o not frown and fret when any task is required of you, but cheerfully carry the little burdens.

SD 149

Man, created for fellowship with God,
can only in such fellowship
find his real life and development.
Created to find in God his highest joy,
he can find in nothing else
that which can quiet the cravings of the heart,
can satisfy the hunger and thirst of the soul.

Ed 124, 125

*J*esus held communion with heaven in song;
and as His companions complained of weariness from labor,
they were cheered by the sweet melody from His lips.

SD 149

*B*ring Christ into all that you do.
Then your lives will be filled
with brightness and thanksgiving. . . .
Let us do our best,
moving forward cheerfully in the service of the Lord,
with our hearts filled with His joy.

CG 148

Above all things,
parents should surround their children
with an atmosphere of cheerfulness, courtesy, and love.

CT 115

$\mathscr{E}$ven in this life
we may catch glimpses of His presence
and may taste the joy of communion with Heaven,
but the fullness of its joy and blessing
will be reached in the hereafter.

PP 602

You do not know how much good you can do
by always wearing a cheerful, sunny face,
and watching for opportunities to help.

SD 149

The Prince of heaven was among His people.
The greatest gift of God had been given to the world.
Joy to the poor;
for Christ had come to make them heirs of His kingdom.
Joy to the rich;
for He would teach them how to secure eternal riches.

DA 277

Faith in God's love and overruling providence
lightens the burdens of anxiety and care.
It fills the heart with joy and contentment
in the highest or the lowliest lot.

PP 600

God has granted men the privilege
of becoming partakers of the divine nature and,
in their turn, of diffusing blessings to their fellow men.
This is the highest honor, the greatest joy,
that it is possible for God to bestow upon men.

SC 79

The sweetest joy comes to man
through his sincere repentance toward God
because of the transgression of His law,
and faith in Jesus Christ
as the sinner's Redeemer and Advocate.

MYP 108

If we are clothed with the righteousness of Christ
and are filled with the joy of His indwelling Spirit,
we shall not be able to hold our peace.
If we have tasted and seen that the Lord is good
we shall have something to tell.

SC 78

True happiness is not to be found
in selfish gratification,
but in the path of duty.
God desires man to be happy,
and for this reason
He gave him the precepts of His law,
that in obeying these
he might have joy at home and abroad.

OHC 63

Seize upon every opportunity
for contributing to the happiness of those around you.
Remember that true joy
can be found only in unselfish service.

MH 362

Those who become new creatures in Christ Jesus
will bring forth the fruits of the Spirit,
"love, joy, peace, long-suffering, gentleness, goodness,
faith, meekness, temperance." Galatians 5:22, 23.

SC 58

God placed our first parents in Paradise,
surrounding them with all that was useful and lovely.
In their Eden home nothing was wanting
that could minister to their comfort and happiness.

OHC 223

God has in store love, joy, peace, and glorious triumph
for all who serve Him in spirit and in truth.

8T 247

Christ's countenance did not wear
an expression of grief and repining,
but ever one of peaceful serenity.
His heart was a wellspring of life,
and wherever He went
He carried rest and peace, joy and gladness.

SC 120

The fact that Jesus died
to bring happiness and heaven
within our reach should be a theme
for constant gratitude.

OHC 63

$\mathcal{K}$ind, cheerful, encouraging words,
will prove more effective than the most healing medicines.

4bSG 95

The religion of Jesus gives peace like a river.
It does not quench the light of joy;
it does not restrain cheerfulness
nor cloud the sunny, smiling face.

SC 121

The presence of Christ alone
can make men and women happy.
All the common waters of life
Christ can turn into the wine of heaven.
The home then becomes as an Eden of bliss;
the family, a beautiful symbol of the family in heaven.

AH 28

Those who dwell upon God's great mercies,
and are not unmindful of His lesser gifts,
will put on the girdle of gladness,
and make melody in their hearts to the Lord.

OHC 63

The Christian is to be joyful in contemplation
of that which the Lord has done
in giving His only-begotten Son to die for the world,
"that whosoever believeth in Him should not perish,
but have everlasting life."

MYP 138

The Son of God came to this world
to leave an example of a perfect life.
He sacrificed Himself for the joy
that was set before Him,
the joy of seeing souls rescued from Satan's grasp
and saved in the kingdom of God.

4T 615

Words cannot describe the peace and joy
possessed by him who takes God at His word.
Trials do not disturb him, slights do not vex him.

MYP 98

$\mathcal{D}$o not be discouraged,
but let your words be such
as to inspire hope and good cheer,
and your influence be of a character to uplift.

RY 68

*B*ut many who are constantly looking forward
for happiness fail to receive it,
because, by neglecting to discharge the little duties
and observe the little courtesies of life,
they violate the principles upon which happiness depends.

OHC 63

God seeks our real happiness.
If anything lies in the way of this,
He sees it must first be removed.
He will thwart our purposes
and disappoint our expectations
and bring us through disappointments and trials
to reveal to us ourselves as we are.

2MCP 649

5—JOY

Are not God's promises, like the fragrant flowers,
growing beside your path on every hand?
Will you not let their beauty and sweetness
fill your heart with joy?

SC 117

The love which Christ diffuses through the whole being
is a vitalizing power. . . .
With it come serenity and composure.
It implants in the soul,
joy that nothing earthly can destroy,—
joy in the Holy Spirit,—health-giving, life-giving joy.

MH 115

*Y*ou can be a blessing
to each other and to those about you.
Be cheerful and happy right where you are;
cultivate the peace of God in your hearts.

RY 68

Circumstances have but little to do
with the experiences of the soul.
It is the spirit cherished
which gives coloring to all our actions.
A man at peace with God and his fellow men
cannot be made miserable.

5T 488

The Christian's life should be one
of faith, of victory, and joy in God.

GC11 477

Christians will not be
mournful, depressed, and despairing.
They will be sober-minded,
yet they will show to the world
a cheerfulness which only grace can impart.

CG 146

We are to cultivate joy and cheerfulness,
and thus represent the Lord Jesus Christ.
He does not want his people
to be mourning and complaining.

RH 28 March 1899

Rejoicing is the very keynote of the Word of God
for all who receive Him. Why?
Because they have the Light of life.
Light brings gladness and joy,
and that joy is expressed in the life and the character.

5BC 1145

The Lord designs that his people shall be happy,
and he opens before us
one source of consolation after another,
that we may be filled with joy and peace
in the midst of our present experience.

RH 27 February 1894

*J*esus carried into His labor
cheerfulness and tact.

SD 149

*O*ur joy
should be in the work of saving souls.

5T 481

The conflict is over.
Tribulation and strife are at an end.
Songs of victory fill all heaven
as the ransomed ones take up the joyful strain,
Worthy, worthy is the Lamb that was slain,
and lives again, a triumphant conqueror.

AA 602

KEY TO ABBREVIATED TITLES

1T, 2T, etc.	*Testimonies for the Church*, (9 vols.)
2MCP	*Mind Character and Personality*, vol. 2
2SAT	*Sermons and Talks*, vol. 2
3BC, 5BC, etc.	*Seventh-day Adventist Bible Commentary*, vols. 1-7
4bSG	*Spiritual Gifts* (4 vols.)
AA	*Acts of the Apostles*
AG	*God's Amazing Grace*
AH	*The Adventist Home*
Becho	*The Bible Echo*
CG	*Child Guidance*
CH	*Counsels on Health*
ChS	*Christian Service*

COL	*Christ's Object Lessons*
CS	*Counsels on Stewardship*
CT	*Counsels to Parents, Teachers, and Students*
DA	*The Desire of Ages*
Ed	*Education*
Ev	*Evangelism*
FLB	*The Faith I Live By*
GC11	*The Great Controversy*
GW	*Gospel Workers*
HP	*In Heavenly Places*
HR	*The Health Reformer*
LHU	*Lift Him Up*
MB	*Thoughts From the Mount of Blessing*
ML	*My Life Today*
MYP	*Messages to Young People*

OHC	*Our High Calling*
PP	*Patriarchs and Prophets*
RH	*The Adventist Review and Sabbath Herald*
RY	*The Retirement Years*
SC	*Steps to Christ*
SD	*Sons and Daughters of God*
ST	*Signs of the Times*
TDG	*This Day with God*
TM	*Testimonies to Ministers and Gospel Workers*
TMK	*That I May Know Him*
UL	*The Upward Look*
YI	*The Youth's Instructor*